NEW-GENERATION AFRICAN POETS

SITA

A CHAPBOOK BOX SET

AN INTRODUCTION IN TWO MOVEMENTS BY

KWAME DAWES & CHRIS ABANI

With special thanks to Martha Mattia
for her extremely generous contribution
to the success of this publication

Published by Akashic Books
©2019 Kwame Dawes and Chris Abani

ISBN for full box set: 978-1-61775-717-4
Library of Congress Control Number for full box set: 2018960611

Akashic Books
Brooklyn, New York, USA
Ballydehob, Co. Cork, Ireland
Twitter: @AkashicBooks
Facebook: AkashicBooks
E-mail: info@akashicbooks.com
Website: www.akashicbooks.com

African Poetry Book Fund
Prairie Schooner
University of Nebraska
110 Andrews Hall
Lincoln, Nebraska 68588

For Lorna,
Sena, Kekeli, and Akua,
Mama the Great,
and the tribe: Gwyneth, Kojo, Aba, Adjoa, Kojovi.
K.D.

*

For Daphne, Michael, Mark, Charles, Greg, Stella—my family.
I love you.
C.A.

NEW-GENERATION AFRICAN POETS (SITA)

Introduction by Kwame Dawes and Chris Abani

CONTENTS OF BOX SET

NEW-GENERATION AFRICAN POETS (SITA)

Introduction in Two Movements
by Kwame Dawes and Chris Abani

PART ONE

The Past and the Possibility of Meaning

In a lively session at the Lagos Poetry Festival in November 2018, a fascinating discussion ensued between a senior and highly regarded poet and a young, as-yet-unbooked poet. The senior poet, with sensitivity but a sense of urgency, lamented the fact that many of the younger poets were not engaged with traditions, were not engaged in the various Nigerian languages outside of English. He was rehearsing an anxiety that I have heard from senior poets around Africa, an anxiety that is sharpened by the fact that much of their own struggle as postcolonial poets and anticolonial poets was fired by a desire to create a new poetics that is not wholly dependent on Western prosody and traditions. The young woman was equally bold in her statement, and instead of railing against tradition, she simply asked, "So whose fault is that? Whose fault is it that I was raised here in Nigeria to only speak English and not to have command of any other language? Whose fault is it that I was kept away from the rituals and traditions of my culture by my family who wanted the best for me? Whose fault is it that I, as an adult, had to enroll myself into Yoruba-language classes so I could speak the language?" It was a compelling conversation about the complications of African modernity, about the sometimes widening gaps between generations of poets who have built at times quite separate notions of tradition.

These conversations can be revealing and instructive about the way that poetry is created and shaped in richly multilingual cultures where the politics of language and tradition nicely complicate the choices writers make. One Nigerian poet who grew up in the north with a father who was not from the north, said she spoke and read Hausa but had no Yoruba, her father's language, even though she now lives in the south. She negotiates her life with English. She says it is not complicated, as most people navigate language through pidgin in its varied and improvisational power. Indeed, as we read work from all over Africa, language is merely one example of the many sites for the exercising of modernity in African art and of the ways in which these writers are exploring ideas of home, of domesticity, of economics, of migration, of gender, of sexuality, without appearing to be working out of a set series of discourses. This circumstance can be unsettling to some, but it strikes me as extremely engaging and revealing in important ways.

It is no exaggeration to suggest that for many of the younger generation of African poets, the tradition that has the greatest immediate impact is the one that is associated with the spoken-word scene that has taken these countries by storm; its traditions are rooted in hip-hop and all of its attendant forces and influences. For many of these younger writers, the embrace of hip-hop was not as fraught with issues of cultural inferiority because they were being bedfellows with black people and black cultures. They have managed to skirt the complications of American imperialism that, in many ways, have come to undergird the discourse of hip-hop's world influence, but that are barely being critiqued by these artists. The great value of hip-hop, however, is the fact that there exist models within the tradition that wholly connect with the politics of resistance, of black nationalism and social progressiveness. For the poets, the slam culture and the spoken-word culture are far more defining and influential than the poetry of African poets of the twentieth century. This has created a peculiar chasm that makes the discussions between the senior poet and this young poet almost inevitable.

My comment on this matter reflects exactly what Chris Abani and I have carved out as our position with regard to what writers write about in this series. I tried to say that I am deeply interested in this debate. I am interested in the ways that the traditions of the past are being challenged and ignored and the ways that they are engaged by a sense that someone may have dropped the ball in the business of passing on a legacy of the poetic arts from one generation to the next. If, indeed, the contemporary society is wrestling between traditional culture and a new modernity, then what we desire are poets with the sensitivity, intelligence, boldness, and capacity for vulnerability to write within that moment. If, indeed, something is being lost, the poetry should enact that loss. If, as is clear, the work of the emerging poets is critiquing the past and the present as well, is engaging in hip-hop but is also fascinated by the outsider discourses of marginality that characterize much of the poetry emerging in America and the UK, especially among poets of color, then it is a good thing to see that manifest in the work. I do think that the alarm over a loss of authenticity is not unfounded, but it is misplaced. The presumption is that the authentic looks a certain way and does a certain thing.

The older poets' desire for the younger poets is fundamentally that they will be proud of their culture, that they will know that their culture has a well-developed tradition of artistry and cultural power and clarity that can rival anything, and that they should not walk around the world like orphans in search of other cultures to embrace them. But what these older poets can't be consistent about is what this confidence will look like. It would be harder for some to accept that this confidence could involve acts that are tantamount to sacrilege or acts that feel compelled to critique these traditions through the prism of contemporary society. At the same time, there is a degree of justification in being concerned that some of the younger writers, in their ambition to "break into" the literary market around the world, have decided to assume the mask of those cultures in terms of their themes, their poetics, and their discourses, and that they have sought to virtually caricature their own cultures (to affirm the view that Western societies have of the African) in an effort to secure the interest and praise of Western culture.

If the Western poetics seem fascinated by the discourse of bodies, the poets will give that world bodies. If the Western perception of Africa is that the men are patriarchal and oppressive to women and that fathers are absent, they will give them men characterized in that way. And if the view is that Africa is a place of conflict characterized by the ubiquity of child soldiers and terrorists, they will generate poems that offer this idea in spades. We are, though, not alarmed at these developments and patterns, just as we are not alarmed because so many African women are writing manuscripts with the ambition to publish, and are, consequently, being published at a rate never seen before in Africa. We are not alarmed because opportunity and exposure offer correctives that are necessary in any literary movement.

Were one to identify an echo that is remarkably consistent across the work that appears in this box set, it would summarize this discussion above in some useful ways, and it would be fraught with difficulties of discourse and ideology, because these poets are consistently positioning their parents—their fathers, even—as synecdoche of some movement toward agency and, more critically, toward an emerging poetics that is refreshingly unassured.

Ama Asantewa Diaka, in her chapbook, locates the sense of tradition within a Christian framework that permeates her work. For her the question of this faith is a place of contestation not rooted in the classic tension between West African traditional belief systems and Christianity (as a Western phenomenon), but instead as a conversation between the traditions of her parents and those of the woman who is emerging now. She thus interrogates the tenets of this faith, and she speaks of the ownership of her idea of self and belief as a departure from that of her mother. In "Let it be" she writes:

> I fret over now and tomorrow,
> giving myself and God a headache.
> Spoon feed myself faith,
> and come up hungry again.
> I have taken up all the space on my mother's prayer sheet
> and the happiness of those I love takes up all of mine.
> At the end of day we're both in God's ears
> saying let it be.

Legacy is complicated. But these poets are constantly engaged with the idea of heritage—fathers and mothers speak, and they are negotiating the troubles of tradition. 'Gbenga Adeoba, in "Child of the world," locates the speaker's sense of self inside the explanation of naming that comes from the father. Indeed, what we see, again and again, in these poets, is an exploration of the extent to which their destinies, as offered by parents and ancestors, are usurped by the circumstances of the present and, more critically, the emergence of "voice" as a sense of individual identity.

> His father said: Son, what you seek
> to drown is not a name; it is history.

His father said he was named
for the rust of songs, scars of Libya,
and the gray vaults of the sea.
He said he was named
for drowned men the world over,
his watered flax and tulips
that didn't blossom,
the dream of years withering still.

Hiwot Adilow echoes this sentiment in her work. In the title poem, "Task of the Prodigal Daughter," she places in fruitful contrast that which she was "taught to be" and that which she is. She transforms the act of prayer into an act based on touching the tangible, the felt, the "real."

I wish I could say I am more than what I was taught to be,
more than hurt rising to the surface to hum
only the chord's cry, the bed left messied,
an expanse of silence, expensive regret.

I know I don't talk to God often,
let His image straddle me instead.
It's easier to hold the thing God made
than admit or repent

Like Adilow, the poet **Dina El Dessouky**, who is of Egyptian parentage, sees her conversation with parents as transgressive, as an act of resisting old patterns and failing to meet the expectations of the parents who are represented in her poem "Food Scraps from the Dining Room":

Mother, I am the worst kind of human.
    I plague your house with
                Bilharzia.

    I plague your house with
             the heresy
                of remembering.

This complaint as characteristic of the path from tradition into the self is equally defining in another immigrant poet, this time **Dalia Elhassan,** who is of Sudanese heritage. She writes of her "father's absence," of the dynamics of family and relationships, but it is clear that for Elhassan, the memory of her father and her mother and her grandparents is elemental to her sense of voice and place, elemental then, to her art. In "jidu (n.): origin sudanenese," she recalls the day her grandfather died and produces yet another uncertain elegy for the "absent men":

> the day my grandfather dies I am fast asleep
> my mother wakes me up and her face is a wash of grief
>
> i wonder what I can say for all the absent men in my life
>
> i don't really remember him,
> just the wrinkle beneath his left eyebrow,
> the *'ilma* wrapped around his forehead

Here, too, is the "heresy of remembering," where remembering is transgressive because the body that remembers is acutely aware of the self—acutely aware of the separation from the past and fully engaged in the process of forging an urgent and present self.

This not only affects the poets living outside of Africa, where the distance from the past traditions seems to make obvious sense, but is also fully present in poets like Zimbabwe's **Charity Hutete**, who, in thinking about her father's legacy in the poem "Worse Than Wolves," finds a litany of what was not told to her as against what was told to her. She must construct her new reality out of the absence, the vacuum:

> He made no mention
> of these quasi-men who bear
> no resemblance to our fathers
> and forefathers, demigods
> who cradled us in calloused hands.
>
> Theirs is a different breed;
> a mutation with unchecked

tongues, wayward fingers
and unmastered man parts.

And in "The Rippers," she writes of the mother who teaches the daughter how to weave—these legacies are constantly foregrounding both the usefulness of the lessons passed on by parents and their unhelpfulness in the face of a world that is changing rapidly. Her art is about reconnecting and separation—a kind of discourse for times of change and betrayal.

Salawu Olajide, a writer based in Nigeria, recognizes that there are rich opportunities for talking about loss and remembering in the story of the West African migrants who make their way to Europe in what has now become the mythical Lampedusa narrative. His collection rehearses this terrain, and in his exploration of departure and return, we are able to see enacted the dialogue with the past and the keepers of the past, who as in other work are the parental figures—father and mother—who are generic in their character but almost always consistent in their symbolic roles. In "Kanako" the father is something of a talisman, a figure whose wisdom helps to shorten the length of the road. But even Olajide is cautious—the capacity for survival is built into the body:

> Father told me this is what happens
> when we dream. Father told me
> our bodies become birds levitating
> through the air. Father told me
> everybody carries a strange city in their body.
> Father said it is where we go when we submit
> to the heaviness of the eyes. Father told me
> Kanako only turns your road into a dream of mirage.

In this way the past and tradition are not static; instead, they amount to a lingering presence that is defined by the uniqueness of the new traveler's body: "everybody carries a strange city in their body." The mother in "After You Left" does not call for return, but she is the keeper of the guide through strange places. The flower she plants at home is meant to guide the traveler as he moves through the world:

> Your mother offers her body to the wind,
> searching for your face in towns
> where geography is learnt by the patterns on
> the palms. After you left, your mother plants a flower
> in your memory, hoping the sun
> will connect the plant and your body.

In "Naming," Nigerian-based **Daisy Odey** opens the collection with a poem that establishes her source, even as she speaks of her own agency in the line "I walk tongue first into myself." But she is named. She comes from somewhere. Her idea of self is troubled but shaped by the engagement with her past, represented by her father and mother:

> At birth my father named me Osun, a place. As I roam
> the world I never leave home. My mother named me
> Oshun, a god. As I pray I hear my voice call out to me
> to save myself.

> A distant aunt says I am like my father, a well, a thing
> that's always hungry. I think I am like my mother, a
> wanderer.

> Together these two things can only birth a river, water
> that never stops running. The shore is a woman; she
> doesn't taste my father in our first kiss. Soon our
> clothes are on the floor, and I think how half in itself is
> still whole.

South African poet **Musawenkosi Khanyile's** collection *The Internal Saboteur* is organized around the narrative of origin and self, and it's broken into three sections: "Father," "Mother," and "Lover"—a love interest that offers the poet a chance to construct a conception of self that is a reflection of the complex wrestling with the memory of ancestry. In this sense, memory and the cultural legacy of a family are foundational to the definition of self later on. As in most of these moments, even the past is fluid and unreliable. But this does not mean it is not necessary to contend with that memory to then address the future. A critical element of the work is how the poet seeks to acknowledge the haunting and sometimes defining presence of his parents in his decisions, and then to start to construct a narrative of separation and responsibility. It is a fit metaphor for the discovery of "voice."

Finally, we find in the poetry of Egyptian **Nour Kamel**, who lives and writes in Cairo, a deep consciousness from the beginning of the work that is establishing a new mythology of self that challenges patriarchal structures. In the poem "Isis in Mohandessin for my Birth," Kamel positions the goddess of the region in a kind of dialogue with the poet's own mother—it is the complex exploration of the meaning of birth that offers the occasion for the poet to consider the sense of self. Kamel's mother is important here but is an unreliable influence—the mother becomes an observer, a witness of the making of this child, and Isis is never a static figure, but one who is pushing against the norm. The movement is from the generic of belief to the quite specific of the poet's self:

> Flew through skies getting too filled forever with
> doomsday shade. Isis, why were you calling after me:
> was I stolen from the underworld by mama's will, or did
> you last minute bless kiss my parts together with pur-
> poseful eyes half seeing a blurred world for what it is
>
> Whatever prophecy you gave, mama said it was an
> omen with worrycast eyes of things to fight unarmed
> vulnerable because they told me I was, all mixed up too
> pale to be born me in the not-moon, who couldn't help
> wage the kind of war my legs meant me for
>
> Women's work women worry women gods! she didn't
> see if it was good or bad, double-glazed reflective glass,
> saw a lost portent of her feathered self something brief
> something that would kill with just a sheath, in silence
> looming, doubled, eat you head, first, whole.

There is something exciting about encountering in these poets not a rejection of the past, but a genuine engagement with it. And this engagement is predicated on a desire to make sense of the present. The past is fraught with contradictory impulses, and yet it offers the possibility of meaning. In many ways, these collections should be a reassuring, even if at the same time unsettling, gift for the older poets who are concerned that the contemporary poet is not engaged by the past—not engaged by the traditions of the past, if you will. What these poets demonstrate is a persistent sense that they have been shaped by their pasts, but they engage the past in the manner of the lyric self. The poetry seems engaged with ideas of the personal, but these are not memoir poems—the personal, instead, is mythologized in productive ways, allowing these writers to therefore "perform" their discourses, which thus allows for the engagement with the rich and complex and competing worlds that are pressing in on their person.

—Kwame Dawes

"Legacy is complicated," to quote Kwame Dawes. Kwame says this in his anecdote about the conversation with an older poet who was complaining that the newer generations of African poets do not, in his opinion, accept or engage with the literary legacy bestowed upon them. This is at best a simple nostalgia and a refusal, knowingly or not, to engage with the true complications of legacy and literature. It is no doubt also textured with the fact that he has, in all likelihood, not read enough, if any, of the body of work he is opining about. This complication might seem obvious, but actually it is not. Even the need to articulate this comes from the experience of attempting to expand, speak to, push away from or against, and even respond to or reject the literary traditions we come from as writers and in the work we make.

The African tradition of written literature is still quite new, barely seventy years old. And when I say "written literature," I am not accounting for religious texts, colonial texts, and reports and diaries. I will account for some of this later, but I am limiting the scope to account for a more intentionally secular engagement based on a writer's desire to communicate with a reader and provide, at least, some basic artistry and entertainment. For the purposes of the work we are doing with these chapbooks to expand and continue a dialogue in literature and culture, I am considering work from the late 1940s moving forward.

This is not to disregard the wealth of indigenous writing systems that populate the continent and have done so for centuries. This includes the better-known ones like Ancient Egyptian, Ancient Meroitic, Old Nubian, Tifinagh, Osmanya, Borama, Kaddare, Mwangwego, the Nsibidi script of the Ejagham, Ibibio and Afikpo of Nigeria, and even recent ones like Mandombe, Bamum, Adlam, Bassa, Bete, Eghap, Venda, Kpelle, Loma, Mende Ki-ka-ku, N'Ko, Vai, Zaghawa, and many others. I have set aside Ge'ez and even Arabic for a different part of these notations. While many of the older forms have been linked to empire and may have been used, as in Kush, Nubia, and Egypt, to write epic poems in the service of gods and kings, they were not used in the composition and dissemination of a written literature. For the most part, literary production in Africa (and in much of the Western world) was up until recently largely the domain of the oral. This of course had to do with the low rate of literacy in written forms across the larger population. Even with the introduction of the Gutenberg press in the West, literature was still oral for the most part. It wasn't written literature that led to the survival of that technology but rather the printing of pardons for the Catholic Church. I say all this to acknowledge the arguments I know this discussion will generate, which, while quite valid, are outside the scope I am aiming for.

The truth is, with the exception of Christian and Islamic empires like those found in Ethiopia, Mali, and Songhai, the writing systems in Africa were largely the providence of male-dominated cults. So, while these orthographic systems existed all over the continent, they were used mostly in religious and occult situations as warnings to transgressors and a secret language within the cults. Some of this was to reinforce the power and fear of the cult, to divert attention from the more power-driven capitalist and (sometimes) bloodthirsty aspects of these cults, and to facilitate trade, such as the trans-Saharan and trans-Atlantic slave trades, as well.

Those parts of the continent—West, East, and North—that had fallen under the conquest of Islam and which had, in an exchange of sorts, received the gift of Arabic and its orthography, used it to produce, or acquire, store, archive, and protect what has been estimated at over a million books. In Timbuktu alone, it is estimated that somewhere near seventy thousand texts remain in existence. Some of these have deteriorated into very fragile states, having been buried sometimes for their own protection. But because of Islam's intolerance to anything not of God, most of these are Korans or interpretations or the work of science—mathematics and astronomy. Yet not very much in the way of the literature we are thinking of, at least when we refer to poets. My only qualifier here is that, since much of this work is not available to me as a reader, scholar, and writer, I can only guess at the content. This lack of access is another matter for the conversation of legacy.

Then there is the case of modern Ethiopia, known by many names over the course of history, home of the oldest Christian Church in the world, and whose religious texts were written in a language called Ge'ze. Once a widely spoken language, it has, like Latin, passed largely into obscurity and is used mostly in scriptural or scriptural-adjacent work. However, the Coptic Church and its officers didn't just write biblical work, in the strictest sense. They created a vast medieval literature that included the myths of the Queen of Sheba and many hagiographies of saints. As with all hagiography, we are confronted with part fact and part myth-making—perhaps an early form of the novel—not unlike the Gothic romances of Europe. For example, the excellently translated hagiography of the medieval female saint Walatta Petros, which contains allusions to what might be a same-sex relationship, reads almost like a novel and should be counted as a form of written literature. When we hear about medieval and renaissance African written literatures, it sounds strange even to Africans, but this is a true and real genre and phenomenon. Wendy Belcher from Princeton University has done a lot of groundbreaking work in this area, and the information is readily available. I encourage you to explore it.

You might wonder why I am writing all this. Rushing through a continental literary history in a quick snapshot? It has to do with the weight and complication of the term *legacy*, and its expressed nostalgia, fear, and an even deeper ache at its perceived loss—one that haunts many older continental writers, mostly men, interestingly enough. I am inclined to wonder though, how wide or capacious their nostalgia is. Does it include all of these contexts, all of these cultures? Does it even account for the orality that preceded the written texts? All of the endless varieties and possibilities of this vast continent, to include all the languages and all the songs? I doubt this very much. In fact, in northern Nigeria there exists, written mostly in Hausa, an immense literature produced by women writers. It is often dismissed derisively as romantic pamphlets intended to spice up the lives of women often living in harem-like conditions. Nothing could be further from the truth. These are novels, often running into several thousand pages, about love; melancholy; loss; gender imbalance; and religious, social, and domestic violence; and they express deep religious, spiritual, and mystical concerns. That these have not been translated into English or any of the other major European languages that are part of the colonial legacy of Africa, much less read, much less assimilated into what we think of as African literature, or the legacy of literature, is a loss, like so many other losses we suffer and have suffered.

It is therefore difficult to speak authoritatively of legacy when we have barely mapped the scope of said legacy. Even in this collection of chapbooks, Kwame has painstakingly tried to peel away and point to the different ways these books are attempting their engagements, and yet—and I don't think he will argue with this—he has barely touched the surface of these ten chapbooks, part of a collection of about fifty such chapbooks we have published in conjunction and conversation with first books, mid-career books, and collected full-career books. The work is vast and only just beginning. We have yet to start approaching all the many African writers whose names are not famous, arranging, scanning, and hopefully creating digital archives of their papers, a stated goal of the African Poetry Book Fund.

What this will yield in terms of legacy will take years to apprehend. Then, of course, there is the problem of translation and the lack of access to all the literatures of the continent, which both Kwame and I have discussed in other introductions. (It seems like the introductions are accounts of our humbling in the face of the work we know there is to do, and the little we have been able to do.) Even with the best of intentions, I am worried that we still think of legacy in terms of a problematic patriarchal heteronormative tradition that is held above most others. Where are the bodies of the queer in that idea of legacy? The bodies of women? Not the token few, but the fully embodied and very empowered women that exist in many oral literatures, or the many female rulers from Egypt to Ife to Kongo?

When we say legacy, what are we accounting for? The many lost languages and thus peoples? Nigeria is a country with 250 known languages, and some of these languages have as few as seven remaining speakers. What then of this vastness? How capacious is this nostalgia that we call legacy and that is often pointed as a weapon against innovation or newness? Legacy is not a static artifact; even artifacts, when broken into fragments and pieces, create new histories in an unending story of place and culture. Neither is legacy a fixed tradition. It is more like a strain of DNA that accounts for all the parts of ancestry but that holds gene sequences we are still uncovering in an ever-evolving process. This is how I think of legacy and the legacy we might be attempting to curate.

Think, if you will, in terms of technology (and language and story are primordial technologies). A legacy is a system that is still in use, many times running parallel to a newer system, which, while paving the way for the new and blending in a way to make the entire system more robust, needs updating and an overhaul. This is what I think legacy is: a verb, not a noun.

A process of creating and recreating and archiving a robust system that accounts for *all* the past, as best as it can. But also is forward-looking. It is the conversation between these two processes, even when one seems to discard another, that maps the way forward.

So then, when newer writers place their imaginations in the cosmopolitan pool that is the African legacy, and expand into places that were silent before, stretching to the point of breaking a legacy, and tradition, to allow the new and the always new but once-silenced aspect of legacy to move to the center in an evolving conversation, then I believe that our legacies are safe and in good hands.

We are and always have been concerned with legacy. We are concerned with archive too, but we are not interested in the form of a classic canon decided by a few people and upheld by patriarchal systems. We are more interested in the living literature, in a living archive, in the verb of legacy. One that continues to define itself in rejection of, and in relationship to, the past, all while projecting into a possible future. The constant living dialogue between what can be, what has been, and what will be.

—Chris Abani

KWAME DAWES is the author of twenty-one books of poetry and numerous other books of fiction, criticism, and essays. In 2016, his book *Speak from Here to There*, a cowritten collection of verse with Australian poet John Kinsella, was released along with *When the Rewards Can Be So Great: Essays on Writing and the Writing Life,* which Dawes edited. His most recent collection, *City of Bones: A Testament*, was published in 2017. His awards include the Forward Poetry Prize, the Hollis Summers Poetry Prize, the Musgrave Silver Medal, several Pushcart Prizes, the Barnes & Nobles Writers for Writers Award, and an Emmy Award. He is the Glenna Luschei Editor of *Prairie Schooner* and is Chancellor Professor of English at the University of Nebraska. Dawes serves as the associate poetry editor for Peepal Tree Press and is director of the African Poetry Book Fund. He is the artistic director of the Calabash International Literary Festival. In 2018, he was elected a chancellor of the Academy of American Poets.

CHRIS ABANI's prose includes *The Secret History of Las Vegas*, *Song for Night*, *The Virgin of Flames*, *Becoming Abigail*, *GraceLand*, and *Masters of the Board*. His poetry collections are *Sanctificum*, *There Are No Names for Red*, *Feed Me the Sun*, *Hands Washing Water*, *Dog Woman*, *Daphne's Lot*, and *Kalakuta Republic*. He holds a BA in English, an MA in gender and culture, an MA in English, and a PhD in literature and creative writing. Abani is the recipient of a PEN USA Freedom to Write Award, a Prince Claus Award, a Lannan Literary Fellowship, a California Book Award, a Hurston/Wright Legacy Award, a PEN Beyond Margins Award, a PEN/Hemingway Award, and a Guggenheim Award. Born in Nigeria, he is currently Board of Trustees Professor of English at Northwestern University in Chicago.

Born in Ethiopia in 1974, **AÏDA MULUNAH** left the country at a young age and spent an itinerant childhood between Yemen and England. After several years in a boarding school in Cyprus, she finally settled in Canada in 1985. In 2000, she graduated with a degree from the communications department of Howard University with a major in film. She then worked as a photojournalist at the *Washington Post*. As an exhibiting artist, Aida's work has been shown in may countries, including South Africa, Mali, Senegal, Egypt, Canada, the United States, France, Germany, England, and China. Some of her images can be found in the permanent collection at the Smithsonian's National Museum of African Art, the Hood Museum, MoMA, and the Museum of Biblical Art. She is the 2007 recipient of the European Union Prize at the Rencontres Africaines de la Photographie in Bamako, Mali; the 2010 winner of the CRAF International Award of Photography in Spilimbergo, Italy; and a 2018 CatchLight Fellow in San Francisco, USA.